THE BLOOD POEMS

THE ALBUQUERQUE POET LAUREATE SERIES

Co-published with the City of Albuquerque Department of Arts & Culture, the Albuquerque Poet Laureate Series features new and selected work by the city's Poet Laureate at the conclusion of their two-year term. Newly appointed poets will join Hakim Bellamy, Jessica Helen Lopez, Manuel González, Michelle Otero, and Mary Oishi as significant voices in the community who have been recognized with the honor of serving as the Poet Laureate and sharing their craft in the volumes published in the series.

Also available in The Albuquerque Poet Laureate Series:

Commissions y Corridos: *Poems* by Hakim Bellamy
Duende de Burque: *Alburquerque Poems and Musings* by Manuel González
Bosque: *Poems* by Michelle Otero

UNIVERSITY OF NEW MEXICO PRESS

City of Albuquerque Department of Arts & Culture

Albuquerque

THE BLOOD POEMS

Jessica Helen López

ISBN 978-0-8263-6325-1 (paper)
ISBN 978-0-8263-6326-8 (e-book)

Library of Congress Control Number: 2021937744

Founded in 1889, the University of New Mexico sits on the traditional homelands of the Pueblo of Sandia. The original peoples of New Mexico Pueblo, Navajo, and Apache since time immemorial have deep connections to the land and have made significant contributions to the broader community statewide. We honor the land itself and those who remain stewards of this land throughout the generations and also acknowledge our committed relationship to Indigenous peoples. We gratefully recognize our history.

COVER ILLUSTRATION: *Zapatista Mama* by Maria Young is an art piece inspired by the Zapatista Movement, the fight for Indigenous rights in Mexico. Also known as EZLN, members of the movement are advocates known for demanding work, land, housing, independence, justice, and peace. The central figure of the mother and child demonstrates what a mother or any parent would do for the betterment of their children's future. The moon cycles are representative of time and space and the long fight for essential human rights. This piece was created to assist in an international awakening on all Indigenous issues.

DESIGNED BY Mindy Basinger Hill

COMPOSED IN 10.25 / 14 pt Garamond Premier Pro and ITC Avant Garde

CONTENTS

As I write this introduction, it is April 2021, and Albuquerque has had Poets Laureate for nine years, beginning in April 2012. To date, five talented, unique, brilliant, and generous poets have been named Albuquerque Poet Laureate— each with a particular voice and a powerful story, each with a special connection to Albuquerque, both the place and the people.

Every two years the administration, selection, and public role of Albuquerque's Poet Laureate is the result of a unique and vibrant collaboration between the community-led Albuquerque Poet Laureate Program (APLP) and the Department of Arts & Culture for the City of Albuquerque. The APLP was established by poets and artists in 2010 to celebrate poetry by recognizing a resident poet who makes meaningful connections, honors and serves our diverse community, elevates the importance of the art form, and shares poetry with Albuquerque residents.

The APLP is coordinated by a seven-person organizing committee that is made up of poets and artists. The Poet Laureate is chosen biannually by a separate seven-person selection committee that represents the diversity of the Albuquerque community and the breadth of the poetry community. The APLP Organizing Committee supports the Selection Committee through a careful review of the competitive applications received and a consensus-based decision process to select an Albuquerque Poet Laureate.

The APLP announces the Poet Laureate with support from the City, and the Department of Arts & Culture coordinates and contracts with each Poet Laureate to implement a community project during their two-year tenure. The Poet Laureate writes occasional poems for the City and is often invited to participate in major City events. The APLP and Department of Arts & Culture both support the work and outreach of the current Poet Laureate in various ways.

Under the leadership of Mayor Tim Keller, the Department of Arts & Culture committed to sponsoring a book series celebrating each of the Poets Laureate, from the first Poet Laureate in 2012 through the present and into the future. We are grateful for the investment by and partnership with the University of New Mexico Press, which brought this series from a good idea to a beautiful reality. Albuquerque's impressive cohort of Poets Laureate has been writing with, for, and about Albuquerque for almost a decade, and we offer these bound gifts of words back to Albuquerque—the place and the people.

Shelle Sanchez, PhD / DIRECTOR, DEPARTMENT OF ARTS & CULTURE
CITY OF ALBUQUERQUE

I PLAY A GAME WITH MY DAUGHTER

My daughter plays a game and asks what type
of plant she would be if she were a plant. I say
succulent, harborer of water even in the driest
times. She likes this and agrees. My mother
is an aloe vera. We agree on this too. My brother Patrick,
a dangerous cactus, poison coursing the needles
protruding from his too-vulnerable, mortal body.
Of course, he is. Some plants were made
from the violence of their surroundings. We imagine
that Angel, my other brother, is a crawling and capable ivy,
clinging to its host, pretty but still a symbiotic and softened
evergreen. My dad is harder to pinpoint and so we skip him.
This is a type of survival. Ignoring him. She says, to me,
you are a tree. I like this and am filled with joy.
For I have always wanted to be a tree. First,
she names me weeping willow and I am too fast
to concur. I imagine my poetic limbs swaying
to the wind, providing shade for the artists
and the lovers. No, she disagrees with herself,
you are too much of a contradiction
for that. You are not a tree after all. You are more
warrior-like. Before my disappointment calcifies she
renames me bamboo. *Mambu. Bamboe. Bambusa.*
She says you are the sound of its own body imploding
when set on fire. You are strict, she says, rigid
in your ability to fight and feed those whom you
love, she says. You are loud, she says, and quiet
at the same time. An incongruence, she
says. So I am a plant after all. No, a thick-skinned
grass. No, a branchlet of harsh weather.
A surviving thing, in any case. And because
she knows the truth better than anyone I know,
I love her the way a mother
loves her daughter.

ONE *The Parting*

SAYING FAREWELL TO NONEXISTENT FATHERS, FUCKBOYS, AND DAUGHTERS WHO MUST SPREAD THEIR WINGS AND FLY

for Mariah, again (Part I)

When we are sieves made of womanly flesh, maternal
muscles that twist and turn in the symphony of our survival.

When all we know is gorgeous, glittering struggle and call
it home. How we hunker down into the nest of our siren songs.

Those fathers and fuckboys who pull our braids, flirt
with the disaster they want us to be and then cut the

twine of our *trenzas* on some nonchalant Saturday night
of their leisure. Damn their lack of oxytocin and chemicals

that makes a human, *human*. And then there is shadow.
And moon. And *coyote* song they never hear. Us, sieves

and sifters of the melancholy. The motherly love of our
boiling blood. The tug of the cervix and salty tear.

When all we are, are caretakers and holders of others' hearts,
so that one day, inevitably, our daughters sprout *shoulderblade*

feathers. Leap and swan dive, torpedo headfirst into the

blaze and chaos we know as life. Though, we know that we've
always known how to say good-bye before we even say hello.

Dear loves, take our spirit with you. Farewells,

our opulent, lavish gift. We a collection of Lazarus rising,
falling and rising again in our knowledge of grandmother

medicine. We a convocation of praying bodies. A choir of escape, captured, found, and fooled. We are your mothers, lovers,

and your best foolhardy plan. *O' men. O' children.* We know how much you want us even when you don't.

OBSIDIAN KNIFE TO CUT THE SHIT OUT

for Mariah, my sister muse (Part II)

When your pussy is made of volcanic glass, lipsharp
and juice of the *blackblue* blood, oozed from the memories
of your *inbetweenthelegs* magic, don't-want-to-remember but
must-not-forget recollections;

You buy a blade. That blade is a root. Is a truffle you were
always meant to unearth. It is a knife to cut
the shit out. Cut the worry. Cut the ties that bind and strangle.
Cut that man's anterior jugular vein. You let the blood pour
into a stainless steel singing bowl. Then boil that shit. Pour
the gelatinous waste from your kitchen window. Let the sun-
shine burn the poison from its DNA.

Then, you cut scraps of muslin, stitch medicine
into the flesh of the cotton. Stitch it
with your pussy hair. Weave the wool of you.

You are your own unrepentant Delilah.

Wield that obsidian blade, sharp and pointed
as a stag's springtime antler free of winter's velvet.

Take that blade and shave your legs. Or don't.
Cut your hair. Or don't. Pull the petrified glass
from between the sorcery of where your thighs
meet. Where your pain sings like a choir of holier-than-thou
bedeviled angels. Glistens with the beauty of your suffering.
Glistens like brine, the way snails and mollusks produce
the fruit of their jelly, propel their muscled bodies forward.
Forward. You will fashion a blade. You will buy a bone-weary
pommel and produce a knife. Carve your name into the nearest
dead tree. Like a good witch does. A bad bitch does.
Cut. Cut the years' past umbilical and bury it
on the east side of your home.

Or eat it instead. Whatever you want, girl.
Whatever you want.

You will whittle a lover from the bark of a cedar tree. Whittle
a friend, a song. Cut the lonely from your rib cage. Cut the shit.
Let the juice of the *blackblue* veins drip
from the old house you once called your body.
And in that house, you will leave the lights on,
let them burn for all passersby to witness the hallelujah of your glory.

For all those gawkers and sin-gobbling capricious folk
to writhe like the summer-tent, born-again evangelical
circus-goers they are. Let them smolder beneath the Damascus
blade that you made with your very hands,
throat-heavy to the touch. Let them judge.

Let them witness how your obsidian
knife is able to blind the eyes. Catch the light.
Refract the phenomenon of sight. Cut
the shit. Bend, girl.
Bend.

The way hematite makes love to the
silica that births the obsidian.

Then, see how they pray,
O' how they will pray,
to the sacred and divine,
blackblue blood–producing pussy.

REQUIEM

I cannot imagine something more fragile than marriage.
—*Valerie Wetlaufer, Conjugal Elegy*

I am drunk again and writing laments for the dead.
Dead eye. Dead foot. Sleep apnea. Erectile dysfunction.

Divorce is a spinning star about to plunge toward its end.
Blackhole. Worm rot. Nostalgia. Misplaced blame.

Dystopia is utopia's more entertaining cousin.
Drama. Heartbreak. Longing. Sorrow.

I signed the papers last Wednesday. The afternoon was alive with sunshine.
Dissonance. Discord. Dismissal. Disappear.

I used to believe in fragility. Now I know that contracts are
an anxious, lying thing.
Signature. Legality. Possession. Liquidate.

I owe the taxman for our marriage. I owe the muse a poem.
Alimony. Child support. Ink. Blood.

I am placing the miles of time between then and now. I am forgetting.
Something new. Something blue. Garter and blossom.

What is divorce if not a merriment of regret? A chorus of *I am sorry*?
Flurry. Exile. The dank. The dark.

I am sitting with Death at my kitchen table,
among the lemon-colored chairs and the cheap
Van Gogh sunflower print glaring down at me
from my white-washed walls. The sunlight is not
unlike the light that graces the face of the Sistine Chapel,
and a gangster rap tune is floating through the neighborhood.

The song is about bitches and how they
all want to spread their legs like the glorious whores
of a Babylonian harlot house. But the lyrics are less artistic
than that, though it has a good beat.

It reminds me of life.

Death is bored. It is listless and moves from one end
of the table to the other, a child hopped-up on Ritalin.

I wish Death would sit still for at least one second.

I want to play dominoes with Death, but it refrains.
It is too busy busting caps into brown-skinned boys from
Los Padillas and Five Points just west of Bridge Street.

I finally catch Death's attention. Say, *Look at me!*
It marvels at my beauty, because I am beautiful.
All the boys say that I am as they run trembling fingers
across my lips. Lips that burst with honey the way a honey-
comb does in the spring. The way boys make you love
them and then leave. As all
boys eventually do.

Death is the male gaze.

I say to Death, *Will you kill me? It's Sunday. The Lord's
Day* and I am melancholy with the mundane chores
a housewife is expected to do. Except I am not a wife.
Anymore.

Not since last fall. *My divorce must be finalized by now,*
I think. But I am too lazy to drive down to the courthouse
and check. Death does not agree with me.

Says, *Divorce is nothing to die over.*

Refuses to hold my hand. How rude.

I will not be inviting Death to
my birthday party next weekend. Take that,
Death. *Let the irony sink in, asshole!* Death
pretends not to be insulted.

Finally, Death offers a bit of compassion. Takes
pity on my young, old soul. Shakes its
knobby-faced head at me. Wags a bony finger
in my direction. *Not your time, darling dear. Not
your time and you must wait like a patient nurse
tending the hospice wing.*

Death is a shroud that shrunk in the dryer.
It is a baby tee. A too-tight pair of yoga pants.

I'll come back for you, says Death. *I can't tell
you when. In the meantime*, Death says, *read a book.
Learn how to cook a green chile enchilada casserole like
you always wanted to. Travel to India or Guatemala.*

*I'm motherfucking Death spelled with a capital D.
I ain't got time for your broken, swollen, flagellating
heart. I've got bigger fish to fry. Divorce ain't no thang but
a chicken wang. Buck up, bitch.*

It then whispers a few other idioms in my direction.
They all make sense, the way Death does sometimes.
The way clichés offer up wisdom of the long-deceased.

And finally, *finally*, I agree. Open the door
and release Death unto the breeze. It swirls
like a pinwheel, or a well-made kite. Free.
Finally free.

And I am a woman ready to write her own story,
drown my sorrows in candlelit operas.

My chakras are whirling, baby.
They be whirling.

THE SMALL TINKERING WAYS I FORGET YOU

At the dentist's office today I did not think of you
for one whole hour. How do I know this? Because
after one whole hour, staring at the neon burn
of merry posters silly with dancing
molars and the insipid sunflower
wallpaper that I hated with such vitriol, I thought,
I did not think of you for one whole hour!

I was alive with this knowledge until I was not.

Among the incessant cuspids, buried
beneath the weight of scented
fluoride, all bubblegum and floating dumb web,

I remembered again
and became a sad thing
once more clutching my purse

alone and in tandem with a flock
of strangers
who waited for braces
or root canals or whitenings,
in the cold hour of that lobby, butts
perched upon fire-alarm red-colored
plastic chairs listening
for our names
to be called.

Listening, waiting,
holding our breath
for someone to finally
say our names.

I found five single socks of yours left behind
the dresser drawer. Last night, I swept and tinkered
away the way a bored ex-wife does after
she has been left. Not quite restless but more
running after her pain with a broom and pail.

One sock was black and donned a hole
where your big toe would have been. It was *paperthin* at the
heel. The white sock played house to a family of tiny,
translucent spiders. They scattered like a gang
of teenagers caught playing hooky.

Yet, another white sock, grey with dinge, wore a dusty beard
a year in the making. It clung to life the way cobwebs do,
ghostly and insubstantial with misforgotten quiet. The elasticity,
a tired bungee cord.

Your Christmas sock was vengeful in its nostalgia.
I hated that sock the most and tried to recall the
last time I saw you wear the wretched thing. I could not.
Holly leaves and whimsical berries danced along
the trimming and this made me sad with anger.

I dug and dug away with my straw broom, carving out
as the wind does packed sediments of limestone and gypsum rock.
Out popped a guitar pick, a stubborn tissue, an old
coupon for triple-A batteries.

Proof that you were neither a frugal nor prudent man.

The final sock hid inside itself like a little conch shell,
balled up and constipated with shame. It unveiled itself
as a prize does, slight hue of azure, slatelike and melancholy.
The color of a rainstorm. I felt sorry for this sock
the most. How it took pride in its loneliness.
How it shrugged its shoulders against the world. How it
calcified in the darkness, buried by the hours upon hours
it had existed behind the dresser, anonymous thing that it was.

A tenderness stirred
in my breast then and I
remembered that I
could be tender.

Forgotten pennies and one nail clipper
had kept the sock company all these long months.

I pocketed those pennies, because
Mother taught me never to throw away
money no matter the denomination.

One day, you may need it.
That night I forgave you
for the first time.

You invite me into your new home, tiny adobe 1907
domicile of Old Town, Albuquerque. It squats in the loose dirt of a
not-quite-ancient neighborhood; small orbs of tight
green grapes cling to the ivy of its birthing along a lopsided
fence that gathers around your new abode.

Hey, here are grapes for you and your old life, you say.
Hold a bunch of translucent fruit into the air,
an offering to the dead.

The grapes are green listless cat-eye marbles, but they cannot see.
Not worthy of wine and not sweet on the lips.

I am as maimed as the summer is, watery light on the horizon.
But still the sun goes on living, limping along.

Seasons change and I am visiting you at your new home,
accept grapes like a parting gift. I cannot help but to receive them.
Later, and you do not know this, I throw them into the garbage,
guilty with a sensuous pleasure. I am shamed with the gravitas
of the loss I feel when
I toss them to the trash.

That day I idle in the new patch of the dying grass of your front yard,
a pallbearer who must at some point go home.
I sense the scent of autumn in the air. It is crisp and dead
as a yellowed leaf. The perfume creates airways
through the nostril and I surmise that some neighbor of yours
is already burning cedar in their stove. It lingers like a soft
blouse in the air. Your new street is ready for fall.

I drive from your new *casita* satiated by my guilty,
morbid curiosity. I shed tears. I hate these tears. Salty
little bitches. It's almost a year since you left. Since
I made you leave. Then why do I stare the way I do at you?
Why stare at the new walls of your new home the way
I do? Something in my bones releases a song, reminds
me that I am newly old.

No matter how mint the ink on your lease is, I recall
the way your belly hair swells around your navel.
It is the last sacred way I held you before our love expired.

Your new home is as big as your shoulders, small as your
ability to understand the way I loved you. The doorway
of your new home shrinks behind my eyes. Recedes into
smallness as I drive away.

So tight and curled over around the neck. Like a question
mark. The way a man who is too big-headed to shove
a shirt over his head struggles
to move in.

Your new home is a gift to both of us.

BLOOD ORANGES

The Stadium Market across the street from my house is selling blood oranges
by the bushel, two for one, three for four, buy five get ten,
and all coupons are accepted.

I load blood oranges into my cart, marvel at the money I am saving.

They become a small pyramid, a piled polygon of my buyer's obsession. A
marmalade of fire warmed during the heated days tempered by cool nights.
Marbled fish eggs, but less glossy than that.
They are Frank O'Hara's favorite painting.

No matter that I could never eat
all of these blood oranges before they spoil.
I am in heaven with all of this blood.
It is a galaxy of pure plasma in love
with the spectacle of self.

I am anemic with the need for the pulp, treasured rind, wine,
and waxen skin. I want to swim in the juice of their sex.
I grab one blood orange and then the next. And the next.

The next. I hoard the blood. I bathe in it.
A newly born spinster infatuated with fruit.

*Chrysanthemin is the main compound found in red oranges, a natural
mutation of the citrus, which is itself a hybrid.*

I am confused with their raspberry scent.
The perfume that lies. I am confounded by
their hermaphroditic ways.
I have not written a poem in days.

I am divorced. I am
hungered. I am.

The distinctive dark flesh color is due to the presence of anthocyanins,
which is also found in purple cauliflower.

I am further perplexed by the science
for that which I crave.

I am a single mother, old maid,
and this the only way
I know how to satiate
my need to hoard, to eat,
to gag the tongue
so as not to spill
all of my bejeweled,
dazzling, dark
and lonely secrets.

THE LESSENING

After all the hatred dissipated, the hatred that carried me through
the best of times and the worst of times, I had nothing
left to dance with. And that was the real empty.
Before, I had my bitter. My guilt and buttery shame.
I had one-sided conversations that rang through the
brain in which I created the fake responses he never
said. The sweet questioning he never heard.
The sobbing animal noises I made that floated up
and into the rafters. For weeks upon weeks, I had my martyrdom.

But then time did its usual. It steeped like a good,
hot cup of tea does. Slowly warmed my belly, exercised
the lungs, and then, of course, came the tide of poems.
The well-written poems.
The globs of nonsense poems. The poems that read like
a preteen's journal. The poems I forced my friends to hear.

Then came the one-night stands. Some good. Some bad.
Some really good. Some really bad.
The therapist bills and hangovers. Then came the wisdom.
The retreat. The tantrums. The defeat. I became
accustomed to the cool pillow and meals made for one.

What I missed the most, I came to realize, was the hate.
For what is one to do when your most prized possession
is gone? No, not the husband. Not the wedding ring.
Not the shared rent. Not the spooning. Not the snoring.
Not the way he couldn't get hard. Not the way he masturbated
in the shower without me. Not the way he
liked pretty girls and guitar riffs but did not like
me.

The hate. When the hatred is gone. The hearty food
I had fed on all those long months. The hatred is what I missed,
that which is not my normal state but became my best friend.
The way I could lean into it, point a finger, snarl at memories and burn
a pyre of photographs in my backyard and call it righteous.

How it held me. Comforted my ear. Pushed the hair back from my
forehead, a tending lover. How the hatred held and held me. Loved me in a way
that levitated my body, glowing warm thing that it was.

One day I woke up and I was not angry. Dumbfounded.
Betrayed at its vanishment. For what is left then?
No one and nothing left to two-step with. No dance partner.
No music pounding in the ear. No oil in the grease fire to tend.
No spatter or scald. No four-alarm agony or lawyers to call.

No anger. And so I sat with my body, my slumped shoulders,
not quite degraded with despair, rather tired with no direction
to shrug. No indignation. No addiction. No victimhood. I awoke
one morning and stared out the window. I stared and wondered,
What the fuck will I do next?

The lack of anger is the loneliest burden to bear.

as if across five seas ten deserts
thirty lifetimes I see you and want to shout
hey I knew you once look at me old friend
you still a groin-tug a mama's belly ache
a womb-coil and relentless birthing
but also a death what love we shared
to know one another the way we did I hope
you read this poem in the very least to know
how deeply we parted how close we still bloom
how I vibrate with peace yet still linger over the passing
how you remind me of a soft grave and always will

TWO *Leap*

ACROSS MUSCLE AND BONE

Across muscle and bone is the lonely highway of the femur, a running
straight shot of calcium and tissue and collagen growing like a revelation.

Growing legs that walked then ran then sprinted quick as lightning from that
small dark house glowing with rage. Growing legs like a sea monkey's miracle
tempered with a child's grace.

I wondered about the body. Me, all protein and awkward angle of pubescent
skepticism, angling toward womanhood and not knowing the burden I was

bound to bear. I grew from a notion that books could save me. That
you would stop yelling one fine day. But your red face never did rest,

and the capillaries dancing around the flared gin blossom of your nostrils
still quiver with an excited anger. Still I grew despite your needing me not to.

I became the puppet of what I thought you wanted in a woman. Then I undid
that folly along the years. Father, holy tree of backyard secrets, how I danced

in the wind for you. How my bone-heavy heaven became your pyre for salvation.
And when I left that empty ministry of yours, eighteen years and swollen with

the scent of my *inbetweenthelegs* freedom, you roared like a tyrant
fallen, toppled statue of bone-white marble. It was the best coup d'etat

I didn't know I had harbored all those laborious years. I grew and grew
into my heaven and it was hell to leave you behind. Demigod. Dilettante.

Dogeared favorite, sad novel. Bone-weary pommel left empty and palms still
twitch with the hunger to own me. I hope you choke. I hope you choke

on the emptiness I left behind. On all of the ways my bones ached with
growth and sprouted muscles and flesh to run from you.

The long grass split in two and allowed my passage. I have found the passage
after all.

FIRE SAYS TO ME

Fire says to me you aren't burning
Fire says I am not defensive, you are
Fire says, I only respond
Fire says, without saying, gaslight
Fire is a gas light
Fire is not water and therefore fire is combustible
Fire is steam
Is endless attraction, is subtle and sexy abuse
Fire reminds you of your father and your first boyfriend
Fire is twenty-five years later and quakes your legs to quiver like a colt
Fire is set jaw, pretty teeth, brown chest
Fire says to me you aren't burning, listen to my fuckboy ways
Fire slithers
Fire blooms holy flame
Fire is your new fad, demigod, fountainhead, fear
Fire be fire and spins your head like a top, dizzy fire
Fast fire
Foolish fire
Fire fueling fire

Fire attracts your inner and outer Aries
War sign and arrowhead

Fire makes you want it, makes you bubble and blister
Fire reminds you that pain is beautiful and worth it
Fire lives
Lives inside of you
You are fire and at least you feel fire, unlike those who can't

Fire writhes

Fire doesn't call when they say they are going to call, or text
Or come over when they say they are going to come over

Fire fucks other women without condoms
Fire fingers you so good
Fire is finger is fire is finger is a fine ass man writhing atop you

Fire is fist
Fire is final
Fire is fickle fire fickle fire

Fire makes you fuck other men without condoms

Fire is the new pandemic, is kissing without regret
Is kissing with too much regret
Is a fire tongue made of flames and broiled mouth

Fire strings you along like a fuse you never lit
But nevertheless don't blow out

Sun-tarnished skin like a ruddy pear,
wood-wind of the Old World. It is a meaty
flesh, tree of crown, five-petaled white wine
flower. *El Rey* of the hardy evergreen. And like
a good vino, I drink you down.

Pear-swollen, simple curve of the left thigh,
where it meets the connective muscle and skin
and sinew and tissue of the rounded ass.

Bosc, Ferrelle, Bartlet.
Brown. Plum-colored.
The cool blue of the shadow.

Down, down, I drink you.
The juice of your perfumed pear
sticky against my lips.

OUR TRANSGRESSION

after Algernon Charles Swineburne

We defiled the neighborhood church park
while the plaster saints looked on from the tip-top
of that cathedral with no bell, bathed in halogen light
cast from the steeple, and your body slung shadows across
the pavement, slim blades of grass sliced into six shades of you.
That night I was sent straight to hell. No matter, I was a willing sinner
half-clothed in old remorse and the newness of a lusty
desirous crime, falling from grace faster than I could breathe.

The slide. The swings. The basketball court and sandbox
where the children play beneath the virginal sunshine of day.
A small sign that read we were trespassing after dark,
hallowed historical landmark.

These little witnesses to our transgressions.
But it was midnight, or maybe 3 a.m., and the moon
was our only judge and jury, cloaked in the black robe of a starless night.

Since I am not afraid of the moon, or you, I bowed
down, down at our altar of flesh and bone and our brown, brown skin.

And all your face was honey to my mouth.
And all your body pastures to my eyes.
Your hotter hands than fire.

Together we sang our own kind of hallelujah.
Hosanna, blessed is he who comes in the name of the Lord.
I am not regretful.

I birth the greasy brine of our would-be vernix, silk-smooth sex
from between my legs and deposit the juice-thick oils
we produce, squeezed from us by the mere viscosity
of our muscled, mollusk-like bodies
into the Egyptian-threaded sheet
tucked clean-tight around my queen-sized bed.

I like the way you are not afraid of what we create,
how you touch it,
talk of it,
fall fast asleep on it.

Not ashamed of it, rather exalt
the meaty, brackish mess of it.
Spermatozoa in suspension.

The next day you drive home, but still I remain,
observe the slick stain, the ointment
thick as lard, buttery dried fleck of biology
that we leave behind. I snap the
linen from the bed, ball the cloth between my hands

and set it to soap in the washing machine. One part me,
one part you. I soak it in water, glycerin, lavender-scented
softener. Down the drain our lovemaking goes, spat into the plumbing that
runs beneath my house, dumped into the city's sewage line,
crisscrossing counties and water tables.

The molecules we induce broke down and guzzled with the tide.
But first it existed in your body, and mine. Waiting to collide.
We are thirty-six views of Mount Fuji and one single, solid thrumming tsunami.

A great wave not unlike the ocean-drunk
painting of Kanagawa,
stormy tendrils and foaming fingers reaching,

blue and lonely as a salty song calling for a shore.

A POEM FOR A

I said good-bye to you with my body.
We were always moving away
from one another. Your chest a barrel,
ripe with red and our passion. I know
your face when it makes love to me, half
grimace, half smile. I sucked in your breath.
You will never take that from me. You can
say good-bye a million times but I hold
you in my gut, my left lung. The blood cells
that oxygenate the nervous system, fibrous
impulses transmitted along the spine like
Tesla's favorite symphony. All light and uncontained
current. Wild orchestra of our machination.
My groin aches with your knowledge and you
are more brilliant than you know. Fire in the sky.
Left behind Hiroshima nuclear shadow, and the trees
weep that they have become cinder.

You are afraid of your own beauty, and for that,
we could never really know one another.
I saw you closer than you saw me.
You saw me closer than I wanted.
You, lightning whiplash of plasma.
Lean with your intelligence, smart
like a slim blade. Sharp as a paper-
cut slice on the forefinger. And the blood
comes later. Two seconds after the injury.

I always knew you would hurt me and for that I wanted
you more. Pain my favorite lover. And you
did not fail to deliver. The hurt you gifted
a delectable, ancient spell. Scientific in its
abilities. In return, I hope I haunt the house
of your blood. At least for a short time.

I said good-bye with my body and I don't
think you noticed. My body a squirming,
seeking length of light. You were blinded by
your own bright wounds.

Still, I do not regret the burns you left on
my thighs, ropey long whips like fingers.
Lichtenberg flowers blossoming the skin.
I invited you in. I delighted in the violence
of our fucking. The blackout drunk
that was us.

I invited the soupy messy alloy of our love,
an impure metal that
had no business fucking with the
white-hot voltage I thought we produced.

The blitzkrieg electricity of me.
The bodysong you couldn't hear,
even though I hummed and hummed
with raw energy. And my good-bye
was lost in the storm. Invisible to the
naked eye. A rogue thrashing of ions,
atoms stripped bare so fast
you never felt it.

AN UN-LOVE POEM FOR THE GUY I LOVE

I am a performance. A high-wire act in a G-string.
I laugh huskily the way you like and sometimes
forget myself. When I do I am all sprawled out
legs and dirty knees. I am crow's feet and gum
in the hair. I am *un-in-love* with you because that's
how you like your women. Loosely attached like a
marionette. Puppet strings and floppy gratitude.

You are every boy I have ever bared my breasts for.
You are new and old at the same time.

I do not say I love you, but I am a thousand
whisperscreams when you come into me.
My brain ablaze with the phrase you fear.

Really, it's me I love. Or life. The way it
expands in my tissued lung, breathes
sideways. A fish of laboring gills. A
schooner tangled in its own sails.

I am a performance but it feels so good.
This high-wire act with no net.
This magician's hat and no rabbit.
This girl sliced in half for all to gawk at.
A miniature dancer moving about like
the frenzied mixed metaphor that I am.

You are all the boys I have ever fucked.
Every boy I have ever written a poem for
or about or by.

I leave you bite marks because petroglyphs
on flesh are sexy. In my own way I *lovehate* you.
I tolerate your disinterested interest. In me.

Really, it's me I hate. Or life. The way it spoils
before the expiration date and my refrigerator
is a constant reminder that I neither create nor destroy;
merely a witness to the meat that rots and the
condiments that pile in my pantry that have nowhere to breathe.
I am the freon that cools the fruit.
Some nights I play you Coltrane. You marvel
at my eclectic taste. Other nights I play you
Snoop Dog, because—well, bitches. Watch how

I twist my yoga hips into sweaty asanas.
You are my audience. My sweet, lean boy.
Other nights I kiss girls I never tell you about.

I *unlove* you. Which is to say, I love you dangerously.
Which is to say, I slice pieces of me like black licorice or
slabs of butter—easy and without grooves.

I am easy for you.

I am the slick side of your bread, homeboy.
I am your favorite *heina*. I write you letters and send them
to the jailhouse of your heart.
No return postage. You ain't writing me back anyways.

I am not fit for your adoration, but I crave it nonetheless.
Your adoration made of false prophecies and promises and
one-sided text
messages.

I am the Marqui de Sade of my own making.
I tie me up and down and don't need your help
to do so. You won't get the reference anyways.

You slippery silt sand dune of a man. When you
hurt me the *puta* inside of me glistens.

Like a little pearl inside a fleshy oyster.
I am lost within your gooey promises.
Your brine and salt, your muscle thick.
Your cum on my belly.
My self-deprecating smile, a beacon.
I am my own conqueror.

Who said I needed you anyhow?
Who said I needed these words?

THE FIRST AND LAST PAIN

after Patricia Smith and Sharon Olds

Ouch. The first pain lifted me into the air,
tossed me like a zydeco tune, threw me
tousled as a matchstick house after the
hurricane struck. It was your posture and I
am a sucker for a straight back and spinal
column like a fine-tuned guitar string. Next,

your voice booming with the hollow sound
of untouched cave. Those eyes, also,
wounded my proclivity and then I was beside
myself. Deep dark onyx and lack of light.

Chest like a billowing sail. You just

tall enough to make me feel dangerous.

How did that swollen moon, the first night we
sat on my stoop and drank cheap beers, disarm
me so? Our knees touching and chests poised
as compass arrows aimed at the heart?
I could taste your tongue before I tasted
your tongue and I knew I was home.

Or thought I was. As if anyone could make a
home while the couch was on fire. The gas leaking
from the stove, a catalyst for the aplomb of a bomb
combusting in the middle of dinner. I tried to
move you in, metaphorically speaking, you
toxic beautiful almost housemate.

Shifty charming man, fickle as a fault line.
But there I was in your arms, brown skin
of the Mexica. That night you drew blood
and I was an altar of devotion.

I am still plucking you from my hair.
I am still unwinding my DNA from your
netted helix. I am still.

There were too many words in our conversations.
There were not enough words in our conversations.

You moved out of my house of metonymy before
you even moved in. I was a bomb shelter. You a false
alarm. I fell to the floor as the war whistles blew,
certain I would disintegrate limb from limb beneath the blast.

My favorite poems to write are about how the
heart fractures beneath the weight of an endless
nuclear winter. My least favorite poems to write
are the ones I lived; in between the spaces of poetic
diction. You know the kind. The kind that drive you

to maddening verse. That drive me to write a sloppy
poem like this. Ouch. This is the last pain and I am waiting
for the winds that will shift this radioactive residue
hovering above my head. For you to leave my house.
The way some men do. Evacuate the city of my body.

Gutted Chernobyl hoping to rise again. For the plant life
to grow again. The wildlife to sniff out safety and
multiply. Again. Populate what was once alive
and then barren. To thrive in the midst of all of this detritus
leaked into the atmosphere. Leaked into the soil and
hopeful water, bright in its shimmering and naive
arrogance.

For the dirt to thicken with the brine that plays host to new
organic life. A thriving ecosystem. This I know can take
years. Decades even, before the first blooming warrior
takes root courageous in its ability to face the sun. Dig
faith-based fibers into a compromised soil. Uplift a frail
chlorophyllic and leafy face, kite-thin and proud.

Maybe a marigold seed. Maybe the taproot of lettuce.
Maybe a foolhardy kernel not afraid to fight for its life.
Maybe mycelium. Maybe not.

It is forbidden to love where we are not loved.

CHIMERA

I may have taken you too soon after my divorce.
But you were a ballpoint pen poised for a poem.
You were slick smile and slanted vulpine eyes,
the way eyes can be sometimes. You were barrel
chest but slim legs and lithe calves. You were large
dick and longevity that took my breath away. I was
hunger. I was Paris. I was a riotous spring. I was decadent,
overreaching words looking for a home. I was older. You were
young skin and I, Maggie May in the autumnal light.

I was ambition and daydream. Long nights and desirous
mornings, afternoons made for distraction. You were
a letter. That damn letter that decimated all reason.
I was a swept-away boat. I was brown skin and pink
lips. You a crooner of Spanish words that stuck to
me like burrs. Purring with poison but still I drank of you.
Plucked you from my skin with a lopsided regret. I was
the day after and tangled hair. I was hangover and grief.

I maybe took you too soon after my divorce. And he,
my husband, was aloof and preoccupation. He was
sleepy side-eyed boredom in the bedroom. He was no cock
and even less love. No hands during sex. No eye contact
during sex. No sex. He was a quiet stone. He was
lack of words and stumbling. He was an apology.

I was boisterous anger and I threw a lamp at him.
A platter of food at the wall once. I was Jackson
Pollock's desperation. I was rabid and lost myself
in a dark forest for many years. I was Van Gogh's
tinnitus. He was a blinded traveler. My husband.
He did not look at me. My husband. I hated not
to be looked at. My husband. My husband.

You looked. You watched. You pounced with a
lusty braggadocious only the young know. You
were an avid museum-goer. You were a ticket-
holder and front-row-seat buyer. You were tourist
and spender of fool's gold. I was too old.
Too careful. Too definitive. Too foolish
to know that you and he were intertwined

between past and present, a chimera of sorts.
Half man and half of a different man. An amalgamated
torso, boomerang hips, sleek hamstrings and
the same type of eyes. I was too foolish to know.
That you and he shared the same lungs.
Same dark skin. Same look-away gaze of the
disinterested. Same trampling hooves.

I took you too soon after my divorce. I married
you too quickly. Years from now I will not regret it,
my proud and clumsy impulses, but today, today,
today, I am a deflated lung, loveless and without air.

POEM FOR MY BELOVED

Part One

For the first time since we've started making love
in my bed, I think of my ex-husband while lying post-coital
with you. It surprises me, and then I lean into the revelation.
You are breathing deeply. You are in love with your recent orgasm
and I don't blame you. It was beautiful. But there I am thinking.
I think of his doe eyes. His big round eyes that were dark and always
earnest, even when I hated that they were so. Now, I miss them.
For a single, hovering second, I miss them. Usually, I am obsessed
with your newness, the desire I feel for you. Where did this thought
of him come from? I don't like thinking of him while sharing the white
sweaty sheets of my bed with you. I push at it. I flail silently as to
not show you that there is someone else in our bed. Then.
I understand that your past lovers are there too. They must be.
Suddenly, I am human again with you. I am so human, I could
burst from my skin. I am so human I want to share my humanness
with you. I don't. I am afraid you are afraid of such things. No,
I know you are afraid. Or don't want to receive such things in the first
place. I push the hair from your forehead with a single
and silent forefinger. Push my humanness away and play
pretend. Again. Again, I pretend.

Part Two

After you left, the next morning I observe the dark and rusted
stains of my period on my white sheets. The way it blots the
thread. It is like chocolate. There is one streak. There, another.
A dead crimson ink blot. I see it patterned like a butterfly
near the center of the bed.
This is a tiny replication of where my buttocks meet one another.

I think it is lovely and marvel at the biology of it. The sheer animal of
my body. The way you create my body feral. I am not scheduled to
start my period. I think you must have pulled it out of me.
You dug it out of my body. You pushed and then pulled with your dick.
Your tremendous gravitational ability to get inside of me the way you do.
You trembled and grunted its way out of me.

Last night, you joked
that you had made me pregnant. You were drunk and uncannily
candid. You repeated this joke several
times. I swatted away your comments and said that my IUD was
most certainly intact and functional,
thank you very much.

Secretly, I was pleased with your inappropriate humor. I don't want
a baby. I want a baby. But the blood says otherwise. It always does.
I bled for you. Was this my uterus shedding life? Or a result from
your violent moon-tide fucking that pleased me so? No matter. I am too old
for babies. Too old for you. Eleven years your senior and I wait
for the axe to fall. For the day you run off with someone closer
to your age. For your fickle nature to shift as the summer monsoon
clouds do. In the meanwhile, I will allow you to fuck me. Or be allowed
to be fucked by you? I never know. You are the erratic response to
my recent divorce. And I am hungry to know love again. Lovemaking
again. No matter how mercurial it may be. No matter
if my blood is an omen I choose to ignore.

Part Three

I like to touch the swirl of hair that surrounds your nipples.
Kiss them to be exact. I like to gulp the air that encases
your brown pliable body. Last night I noticed a new mole.
I forgot where it exists. Was it your chest? Your neck?
The energy confounds me when I am near you and so
I forget all the things I want to remember. I like the way
your saliva swirls upon my taste buds, milky gooey galaxy
of spit. The way it sits on my tits, suspended dew drops
produced by your mouth. It is sweet
with something I always forget. I always forget.

When you are inside of me I am dizzy with pain. When you
are beside me I am dumb with wont. I am always neglecting
some detail. Maybe this is the way I survive you,
never letting your memory rest. How many times

must I possess you before I let go of this wrenching, rendering
thing between us?

This liquid obsession is no friend of mine but still I reach
for you. I like to touch the back of your neck. Pull the cords
of its muscles like a kite in the breeze. Try to reign it in.
The black hair of your head is a glistening helmet. Hermes' winged
petasos. I can't seem to understand the lure of it. How it holds me close.
Captures me in its deep jetty hue. Where is my will?

It has flown up beyond my body. I am creature
in need of glutton. A wounded body. Oh, silly silly me.
I am a creature pulled into
the habit of writhing to the tune of your ocean.
I drown in all the ways you wash over me. I am creature
and creation and spark of dust.

Part Three and a Half

I look at you the way you want me to see you, at first.
You are a young swift man whose heart is a glittering, golden
globule. A boy with too many crushes. Maybe too many unintentional,
sweet-fattened lies? Like *dulce* on the tip of a melting tongue.

Then you are a letter. A crude ink-scrawled poem upon the
pages of vanilla-hued paper. You are a better writer than me.
I am jealous and in love
at the same time. I am in love with my jealousy over
your talent for writing. This makes me wicked with pain.

I see you as a lopsided *payaso* and know
I am a wrong angle. You romantic thing you,
with a mathematician for a heart. All logic but brimming with
every possibility, the way geniuses usually do. I look at you
the way *she* might have and I can't bear the comparison. I am
too territorial for my own good.

I am too mad like a hatter with her sewing needle. I stich
you in the shape of me. It does not work and so I revise the poem
I have sketched for us. You are fickle. No. Not that. You are fleeting.
This is an ill-fitting robe. You are wild and untamed. I like this better.

I cannot find who I think I might think you are and so I still
marvel at your mysteries. Yes, this will do for now. I try
not to look at you the way I want to. My perception too
sullied. I would rather wait for your surprises at the door
of my house. Wonder at your newness. Stay in the uncharted
waters of your presence. I hope I never know you.

Never know you, I hope, and the pain is a palpable saturated thing.
I want to be enthralled by the dazzling light of you for always.
Let us be young forever. Stupid and traveling without a map.
Sun-drunk and lost in the rays of the blinding sun. Let us be
strangers for always.

Part Four

The black-and-white portrait of you is a compass.
Your lips, bow and fiddle. Your almond eyes hooded
and inky with an ebon knowledge. There is your young
chest, your vibrant neck. Skin without pores and silken
to the touch. It is not yet ruddy with age. I inhale your
youth and feel guilty for it. Your intellect is a beacon
and I witness only a partial glimmer here and there.
It is too big to understand and I buckle at its altar.

There is your bravado. There is your angled jawline.
There is your neckline I like to lick. There it is.

I have never written this many poems for anyone.
What is this? I will go on and on with my words, I think.
I read too much of Neruda and Olds and shipwrecked Marquez and tragic Lorca
and the crude Bukowski and the sexist Santiago Baca and the lovelorn
Cervantes and horny Cisneros and illuminated Wakoski and pornographic
Anaïs for my own good.

I read too much sleepy, half-eyed wistfulness. I grow too large
with your love. I think, you are a lucky lucky man that a poet
has fallen in love with you.

Part Four and One Quarter

I can hear your voice in the bell of my chest. It echoes
like a lost buoy. It chimes. It melts with sound. I am
a helpless target. I dare not say I love you/love the idea of love aloud.
The syrup of my silence is my favorite seduction.
But if I could, I would *murmurmurmurmurmur*
my devotion into your ears. Instead I write poems
days after you leave my bed. Keep the fire alive
with words best whispered into the verse of my desire.
I want to choke you with my long, dark dark hair.
The longing of my favorite obsession. Watch how
your photo transforms beneath my gaze. Watch how
I uncurl my blood beneath your body. I bleed like a felled mare.

Part Four and Three Quarters

Last night your face was inches from mine and you dozed.
Lips parted slightly and your breath was a sweetened
dream. I popped an eye open once or twice to watch you.
How close your nose was to mine. How your eyebrows
arched like a quieted symphony. Then we shifted bodies.

You grazed your hand on my thigh. Still you slept.
A prized possession and I was fascinated. Our nude
bodies susurrate with our lovemaking, moist with a maddened sweat.
I was a livewire. Sleep did not come for me. Instead I listened for the sound
of your body's mechanisms. How it toiled. A peaceful
young man in love with dreaming. Still and unmoving in its
beauty. This is the meaning of love, whatever that
means. A love I will never name aloud to you. Instead
I hear you breathe. Wait for the next time our bodies
celebrate this thing called life.

Part Four and Whatever Comes after Three Quarters

Your brown body against my white sheets.
Fingers like a composer,
the watch that graces your wrist, an ode to your intellect.
Your brown body against my white sheets.
That smirk, that unconscious tick and the way you repeat
what you find funny. Your humor a precious metal, a thing to be coveted.
Verbatim and husky with amused
delight. Your braggadocio. Your dick. Your hip.
Your thrust. Your pull.
Your laser-sharp wit. Your brown body
against my white sheets.

Your brown body against my white sheets.
The mound of your buttocks, your back of thigh pressed
against a pillow. The way you press.

Part Five and Some Change

Your grunts and groans.
Your red-faced orgasms. Your mumbling during our sex.
The way you force yourself into me.
The way you take your time.
The way you ask without asking.
The way I say yes without saying yes.

I am split open. I am yours.
The way you know this.
Your brown body against my white sheets.

Your mouth like a honeycomb.
Your slivered eyes like dark almonds
Your eyes, your eyes, your eyes.

Your barreled chest and the way you thrust.
Your flattened young stomach. Your hips.

And how they meet the length of flesh and femur.
Your brown body sweating against my white sheets.

Your pouty and parted lips, how they sing for me.
How they dance across my chest.
How you take my small breasts into the weaving fingers
of your hands.
Your hands, your hands, your hands.

Your body hair that sways and eddies like little rivers.

Your river.

Part Six and the Swan Dive

Your brown body against my white sheets
Your brown body against my white sheets

Your brown body

This is the only way I know how to write of love.
The only way I know how to swallow
the lust you enkindle
inside of me.

How I don't yet know how to say
good-bye.

How my thighs undulate.
Ululate. Still.

How still I compose words
for you.

How I write poems for you.
Still.

Part Seven, I Think

I no longer love you.

I have traveled against time to finish this poem.
I am drenched with relief.

I realize it was never
love.

It was love, but I'll
never admit it.
It was fire in its finest
fuckable form.

I think of no
one else
since you.

You tell me that there is another woman
who haunts your blood and she is a shadow,
months removed. I take you for your word and
wait like a patient in the cancer room not sure
of my next diagnosis. Skin cold and prickly
but still I sit in a paper robe while you wrestle
with the old voice of your old lover. Or so you say.

I think I am in love with you. I do not say *this*
aloud, because I am smarter than *that*. Instead,
I count the cracks in the ceiling above of my bed where
you have left me naked and wet and waiting.

You leave. Come back. Leave again. Come
inside of me. Leave.

We did fuck once or twice in your home, but
mostly we do it here within my white walls that
encase our moans. I used to make love to my
husband on this bed, but I never mention *this*.
I am smarter than *that*. I am smarter than *this*.

Besides he is long gone and I no longer see
his face in the mirror behind me when I brush
my teeth or comb my long black hair that has grown
longer since he has left. I've made my amends.

You said good-bye to me last Sunday. The summer
breeze whipped through my window and the curtains
danced around your head as you sat upon my dining
room chair. A white crown of flames drunk on
its own beauty. You, framed in all
of that billowy fabric and I knew I would remember
it for always. We spoke in hushed and peaceful

voices as if we were planning a lovers' vacation.
Hopeful, flirting still and saying more with our
eyes and hands than our words. But what of it?

My heart fluttered for a second, the way hummingbirds
do, right before they drink the nectar. The way *huitzils*
dive bomb into the blossom. It was a sweet pain
and I knew what you were going to say before you said it.
But my hope prevailed, which is why it hurt the way it did.

You said good-bye. You ended us. And I nodded like a
priest does when a sinner confesses, full of righteous
acceptance and faith that God will not judge the wrongdoer.

My mind said, *no, no, no.* But just barely and it was not
at all perceptible to you. And like a cloud over a placid
lake my heart shifted into the idea that it would soon dissipate.
The way clouds do. This is the nature of them.

For what could I do, but dissolve? We exchanged a few
more smiles, light laughter, and wit. I shed a few
tears. They wet my eyelashes but nothing more. They did
not fall down my cheeks. I would not allow *that.*

You tell me there is another woman you are no longer
with but she is still present in the chambered halls of your mind.
I know *this.* You have mentioned it several times. *This*
time I listen. I am soft with my ability to understand.

I have never been so patient with love. You will not return
this time. *This* time, never again to return. Still I hold you dearly
as I let you go. *This,* how strong my heart aches for you.

THREE *Changeling*

I was always meant to wear the red dress, dripping with my breasts.
Brown-hued halo that it is. I was meant to squeeze my ribs into corsets and
crunch my waist into small cubes of flesh squared. I was always going to dance
in heels and pay the price, calf-cramped and aching toes the next day. My lips
were never not going to be painted red-light district *red*. I was your daughter, father.
Your wishy-washy delight. Mother, you always meant for me to be dutiful,
stiff-backed and bent
head over *his* and *his* crotch, legs splayed as an offering to the empire that
is *man* and *men*. I was always going to bellow, stomp my keratin hooves and flare
both nostrils until they became deep and dark caverns, bottomless black pits of
heated breath. I was meant for this bridled red dress, these crystallized sins, long
legs ropey itching to trot.
Tear away into the wind. I was a wild horse woman, bearing a bare-back Athena
until she left me for the siren song of war. Half woman and half of another woman.
I was always meant to be stitched in tatters by the red dress I grew out of. I was
always meant to transform, sprout the equine muscled torso from my human chest;
the feral mane of wiry rooted hair from the head. I was meant to whinny, rear back,
buck and neigh, flail like a wild thing, undomesticated Tarpan, *equus ferus ferus. You
will know me by the red swatch tethered to my lean and fleeing flanks. From the way I
don't allow anyone to pull, reign my hair. Anymore.*

Transform. Transforme. Trans.

Every night a wolfdream.
Every night a howl and backache.
Every night and morning a six-pack of pain.
Every night a wolfdream on the tip of the tongue.
Every night a magical house on fire.
Every night and every night a flame.
Every night I wake from a sweating grabbing thing.
A slithering but sometimes also light, floating orb,
cool touch on my forehead.

Last night I dreamt of a slanted wall that my mother slouched against,
she saying *sorrysorrysorry* about whatever it is that has me dreaming of wolves.
Wolves of slathering teeth and watery eyes and fermented blood and itchy skin.
Every night I remember and every morning I forget.

Every night I dream of a wolf running back to the pack.
Its receding haunches and fiery hair lit with electricity.
Running back into the swallowing night, letting me know
without letting me know to leave the howling
where it belongs;

how it belongs to the hot and secret night.

MY EARRINGS TURNED BACK TO WATER AND TRICKLED DOWN MY SHOULDERS

after Angela Carter

I.

An apology to the wolf, that I a small girl should rush into the fear-dripped night and blame it only on him, when really it was a tide of women who did it to me. Held me down to let me bleed between the legs. Gifted me the heirloom of acquiesce. It was not only you, dear dead-eyed wolf with the yellow gaze, hungry for what you were born to eat, snuff out, destroy. But the women too. The mothers and the grandmothers telling me to sit still. It will only hurt for one small trickling moment. In the end we all become water, bearer of glistening reflective pain, again. Again, we always become the water. Sliding back into the earth where we women belong. Into the crevices of limestone and cracked earth, deep down where we aren't remembered until we are explored. Discovered. A flag planted in our breastbone. Cartography outlining the conquered territories of our bodies. Here is a fairy tale.

II.

In the shadowy mirror of a shallow lake, silver and quivering with the reflection of the moon, I became energized with the gothic horror of life, which is to say I finally saw and became beauty. I sprouted feathery haunches like the wolf, bristled like a mare with nostrils on fire, steaming opaque tendrils of red-hot flames bursting from my snout. I was the bridled bride, the dismembered *huérfana,* the broiling sinner. Icarus and his stupid father. A Mexican Medea. I scratched my eyes from my sockets, but not before I held my children beneath the currents of an aphotic river. I gave them a watery tomb and cursed my lot for good. If this is pain, thankfully I am a writer, a poetess submerged in the image, the rotting ivy-clinging image. The feigning folklore. The paint and porcelain of earrings turned back to water and trickled down the shoulder. Apologizing to the wolf, because the wolf is me. The wolf is me. *Lo siento.* Here is a *dicho.*

III.

I take refuge in the veined bat-winged lopsided truth of the night. Between two swaths of darkness, one darker than the next. I am at home. I can set flame to this city, rewrite the outcome. A wandering and pondering motherless child. Here is a fairy tale.

MY BROTHER'S BRILLIANCE

If my brother's brilliance could write a poem, it would read:

Bipolar alcoholic manic depressive homeless guy who hangs
out on the corner of Pine and Pearl Street.

You would know him as the bard of:

I carry a leather handled suitcase from St. Ann's Catholic Church thrift store,
and yes my wrinkled shirt is this bright and pink and distracting.
Lots of times I am actually funny. This is a sign of my genius.

What you may not know is that he used to:

write poetry infused with a soft and subtle tongue cushioned
with hip-hop lyricism, lush with coy entendres and alliteration that could
dazzle the mind. He was able-minded. Once.

My brother is repentant but does not often vocalize this. If he could, he would say:

I left my young son to fend for himself. I love him but
I could not care for him. He roams the streets and his name is Alejandro.
He dropped out of school and hops city buses traversing here and there.

He would repeat.

I have a son. I had a son. I had a job. I owned a car. Had a wife. I had a son.

If you ever have a conversation with my brother, and you just might
for he is a gabber, a natural with words, friendly until he is not, he might say
to you:

How are you? I like your shoes. Tell me about your life. I am interested and
compassionate despite this grime I carry, oiled and blackened like a dirtied oven,
burdened with years of use and no companion to help me get clean.

If you asked my brother a certain question, a very specific question, this is how he would answer:

It was my father, and my mother
too.

He would say:

It was both of them
who did this
to me.

DREAMING OF KILLING MY BROTHER

I dreamt I almost killed my brother. Last night
I dreamt this. That the silver gun was alive in
my palm and I checked the barrel for bullets.
How did I know how to do this? Dream knowledge.
I've never shot a gun and I have never killed a brother.

Last night I was ripe with murder. He was rampage.
The way he is when he is drunk, which is all of the time.
Like the time he spat in my face. Threw a rock at my window.
Smashed my car with a bat. Called me cunt.
I, a woman on the verge of blood, almost killed him
last night. He's a drunk.

In real life and in my dreams. He is danger and the homicide
that accompanies cheap vodka swilling with madness and the lust
for death only a drunk knows. He has a lazy eye.

In real life and in my dream.

When he was a boy my mother slapped a patch
on the good eye so his weak one would learn
how to be stronger.

It didn't take and he knocked about the house,
blind and only three years young. A pint-sized cyclops.
Lamps shattered. Dogs howled as he trampled
about, slamming into their bodies. My dad
played the radio louder and cracked open beers.
This is how he drowned
out the sound of his children.

Last night in my dream, my brother was a red-colored
threat, the sound of an upturned rattle a predatory snake
makes. Poised for the strike.

I never saw my brother. In my dream, that is.

But I knew he was there breathing in the other room.
He was coming for me. He was coming to tell me

all of the secrets of our house. I yearned for silence.
To shut his gaping and suffering mouth. To forget that
he is now homeless and wandering the city somewhere.

In my dream and in real life. He is a blinded leviathan,
holding all of our family's tragedy in his belly.

Like the way my mom used to be a black-out drunk who peed herself.
Like the way my father lipped a crack pipe not unlike the way
one French-kisses a lover.
Like the way I left home three days after my high school
graduation and never looked back for him. The way I left

my little brother, blind and forgotten, destined
to cradle the bottle the way a father might hold a child.

I dreamt I almost killed my brother last night,
and I felt like it was my duty to do so, without guilt
and ready to pull the trigger. I was ready to pull the trigger.

And then I woke.

BROWN GIRL IN THERAPY

after Ebony Isis Booth

When you leave therapy in tears, once again, driving 95 mph/
down the I-25 for the second or fiftieth time/you begin to question
if your hard/fought-for expensive-as-all-hell/insurance is worth
the trauma/because you can't remember, not even one time/
you felt any better because therapy taught you to smile/and all
you know/is that you are driving too fast/for salt-soaked blurred vision/
and she is blonde and blue-eyed/and the lead intake psy-/
chologist told you that she is a good fit for you/but you know it is only
because she is woman/and that is all she sees/and she is at least fifteen
years your junior/her eyes are so damn blue/blue and clear and wide-
eyed and innocent/nothing like your own/then you feel/sorry/
for her/talking of blood and crack/and how Compton broke your
father and this is why he is cold/never mind the time mom's nose
was smacked wide open with his palm/and you were
only baby-soft and ten years old/so you cry when you don't want to/
and she nods and passes you a tissue box/you notice it is not a generic/
brand and wish it were/because at least you would feel a bit more at home/
at the sight of discounted accoutrements that remind you/of a home
that never really was/a home/in the very least/so you pay the damn bill
that comes in the mail two weeks later/vow to never return/never to drive
95 mph with salt-stained eyes again/instead write a poem you never/
neverneverneverneverer want to publish/anyways/and don't go back
to therapy/that's for damn sure/even though she has framed
her scrolled diplomas and hung them/on the wall/and they remind you of little
sheets of curled flesh/and this is because only white
girls/relate to that type of bullshit/and in the end that is all
that it ever was/anyways/bullshit/and no one ever told her/that brown
girls love/their pain more than they love themselves.

THE PHONE CALL

Future together, you say we have a *future together*.
Brother and sister fused, amalgamated relations and over the phone
your breath is a desperate wind. I can hear it from here, four hours away, 233.6
inky and lonely miles from my hometown and the place where I now live.

Still the distance is not enough. The 1,233,408 feet. The 411,136 yards
cannot lessen your tug and request of that dark favor.

You on the phone, when pay phones still existed, and the traffic around me billows
with a lusty and *gasdrunk* exhaust. I think, for a split second, *what could go wrong*
and think too, *everything will go wrong.*

His lazy glassy eye, dark horse of a brain, bald head and miniature ears
like little bookcases holding together the gray matter of his narcissistic needs,
my father's, *our* father's, glittering violent heirloom of self destruction, storm of
rainingdownfists on the back of my brother's head. All those years.

This even before my brother took to the bottle and we didn't
know what was in store for us, for him. All the wet days yet to unravel.

You ask me if he can come live with me. I hear your weary windpipes release
a final battered *breathrattle.* And I imagine you holding, holding
onto the receiver as if it were an anchor of a *stormtousled* boat, waiting for a *milagro*
to rain down upon you.

I love you so much that I say yes, before I hear myself say yes.
I pity you and so say yes,

Send my brother to me. He can eat of my food. Sleep on the misshapen couch
of my roomless studio. He can drink of my breast and break all of my cheap dishes.
Laugh like a maniacal machine, his voice forever echoing into the night and out into
the courtyard of that tiny one-bedroom, brick-and-mortar complex.

If you visit there, we are still there, two ghost *adultchildren* learning how to die.
I hear if you visit there the renters listen for the squeaking *mousebrain* that was his,
the turning machinations of my fever dreams. How I tossed and sweated into those
sheets, the cantankerous furnished bedroom.
His voice still claws and clamors inside of the walls. Vermin writhing, scraping
a way out, scratching against the plaster.

One of us is crazier than the other.

I was a mere child myself, skinny flat-chested waitress hopped up on tips and cheap
afterhour booze, sleeping my through men, one ear cocked for my father to call me
home.

And so I say yes to you.

I, survive this city for many months but celebrate each and every one
of my losses. I, who am made of something more than lack of vertebrae and jelly
limbs.

I, who am tempered steel and a synonym for survival.

You know this and so you ask.

I can pull him to shore, I think. *I can help him float.*
I think.

Yes, send me my brother, I tell you, Mother.
Send my brother to me.
And the big city
whirls around, kaleidoscope of all shades black.
A monochromatic traffic jam. A sightless corner street.
A tomb. A wish. A hopeful star.

I will feed him. Hope he doesn't burn down the apartment.

Alive with only two decades of wisdom, brimming with rage and sugar-spun
pipe dreams. I believe. I believe.

I will do my best, Mother.

I will do my best even though I know failure is ours.

A big sister holding little brother's hand and walking into the crest of desire.

I cradle the phone receiver, hear the operator,
when operators were still a thing,
tell us to insert more coins,
lest your lifeline be disconnected.

Hurry, hurry.

But I have no more change to give, my pockets silent
with the lack of the *madjangle* of currency. Barren burrowed,
burdened deep holes burning into my thighs.

And so the phone goes dead.
And so the phone is a silent snake alive in my hands.

SOME INSTRUCTIONS ON HOW
TO KEEP THE MANIA AT BAY

Here is what not to rejoice: marriage and divorce.
The mangled rubberneck crashfuck of it all.
Childhood. Adulthood. The in-between.

Here is what to marvel: children born of the fist.
Tiny heads and genitalia and little toes. The way
they love you before you know how to love them.

Here is a misfire: your father. Your mother loving
your dickface of a father. Your brother wrecked for life
because he loved your father. The guilt and success
you experience because you did not love your father.

Here is how to fake loving your father:

Take this stone. Put it in your pocket, your mouth, between
your teeth. Chew and spit out the agate of your hatred.
Let the stone melt to sand. Let the sand call you home. Be violent.
Always be violent. This is how you protect yourself.

Lie about the ways you are intimate with violence.
Hide the violence.

Offer yourself: this is post-traumatic
stress disorder. This is nonsequitur relief.
This is not making sense even in the best of times.
This is why you are a good poet.
It reminds you of belt buckles and empty fridges,
your father's drunken hair.
Hold your fists in front
of your mouth. Knuckle your lips.
Hit anything that is soft.

For the rest of your life don't be soft.

You are still writing these poems: off-putting, stale,
loveless milk whiffs and lonely Easter mornings. Mom is drunk.
Dad is drunk. You and your little brothers raid the empty
fridge. Write a love letter in macaroni.

Here is what not to rejoice: an editor publishing
your poem because it is fraught with truth and asymmetrical
diction. Keep writing. It is the only rebellious mania you know.
Editors adore your raw and unfashioned form. You don't have to.

Take this empty bottle: move to Paris. Watch your daughter
graduate.

Move into the empty bottle. Tuck your limbs into the glass corners
of a rounded bottle. Be the bottle. Drink the bottle clean, dry.
Drink until you are forgetful drunk.

Make a circle into a square.
Make the bottle into a neat and tidy home,
burnt amber–hued glass.
Hide in the opaque. Move to Albuquerque.
Move to Tokyo. Move to Managua. Drink the bottle.
Always drink the
bottle. Clean.

Clean. Clean. Clean.

Blanch at the way truth sounds, the way your therapist talks.
Your guru. An Al-Anon meeting and the way it syncopates
into a choral lament. Like the Western World reading a self-help
book at your funeral.

Blush at the sound of the word *abuse.*

Hate yourself for knowing that you were abused.
Don't tell anyone you were abused.
Tell everyone you were abused.
Regret the telling of your abuse.

Repeat. Cycle. Repeat.

Here is how to blush: when your father tells you how your
body is tormented. How your awkward breasts disappoint.
How your belly is too big. Your legs too thin. How he knows
you got dick last night because of the way you walk. How the tip
must have slipped

in. How your little brother laughs at this joke.
How your other little brother drowns his sorrow, too
drunk to notice. Drunk enough to notice.
How your mother ignores. How she walks to the back room.
How she takes refuge against your battering. How she always partook
in the abuse by walking away. How you chew on your lip and stare at
the ground. How you laugh too just to make it go away.

This is them not recognizing your grief. This is your
embarrassment at how you used to but can no longer
call it out. The fatigue is a foggy thing. This is them silencing
you.

This is flint and your skin is on fire and you got used to it.
This is you frying and no longer feeling the heat.
What is heat anyways?

This is you ashamed, and the little girl is confused
by the big, bad sexiness of it all.

Here is how you hide your chest: make sure you wear a
bra when he comes over. No shorts. Never shorts.
No cropped tops. Never cropped tops. Your hair is pulled back
into a bun. He hates buns. He hates. He hates. He hates.
Hide the outline of your nipples. Hug sideways. Don't press
chest to chest. No kisses on the lips. Keep your distance. Here is
how to hide your breasts. Hide your breasts by any and all
means necessary.

Here is your mother telling you, *Well at least he never beat you.*

You are a bullet: dead, right after the trigger is pulled.
A spring mechanism, a pin and a cartridge, a gun primed
to explode.

Read this letter: *Dear Daughter, don't be a slut but be
a slut otherwise you will disappoint. Here is Hustler and Penthouse
and Playboy. Here is how I think you should pose. Pose, bitch,
pose.*

Hillary Clinton is a bitch.
Your mother is a bitch.
Your mother's mother is a bitch.
You are a bitch.
Therefore your daughter is a bitch.

Here is how your mother limp-wrist excuses it all away,
His mother died,
and, well, I felt sorry for him.
I like when he cries. I can see his human.

Here is what not to rejoice: your father. Your ex-husband. Your baby's
father. Your alcoholic brother. Your other brother who laughs.
Your mother who ignores. Your daughter who watches on.

Your father. Your father. Your father.

Your accidental joy at feeling nothing at all.

A LETTER FROM SAD GIRL

Querido El Duran,

It's me, the spirit of *La Blue Eyes de Eco Parque.* The not-quite *guera Mestiza morena* with the sad look and big brain. Poetry sleeping in her bones, a *calavera* midnight madness. My homegirls cut me slack, though, know that I prefer books over brawn, *murales de arte* over *placas y pistolas.* I am the one who runs wet fingers over your letters, the ink an indigo weeping. You who I squeeze between the onion-thin tissue of envelope, skinny lines of dollar-store stationary. Bubble hearts and lopsided roses drawn in the margins. My tongue is scissored in papercuts and cheap glue. Dated stamps and postal service zip codes. *Did you get my last letter?* Like I said, my homegirls cut me slack, though. Don't give me shit when I don't come out for a Saturday night cruise beneath the beltway of Route 66 stars, beneath the eye of a hungry desert moon. Don't give me shit when I don't meet them at the swap meet to buy bootleg brands, knock-off purses, 99-cent nail polish on the cheap. Don't give me shit when I linger along the *Rio Grande*, searching for your face in the muddy runoff of her watery womb. She is an oracle and I look and look to see if you really love me. Always my response, a gurgled whisper, a cottonwood dream, hapless currents without destiny. Anyways, she answers me the best she can, in riddles allllllll lopsided in their fluid meaning. Choked out by *acequias* and water-right wars.

I do my best to hold on to Sundays. These days. This is when I get your letters. Sometimes.

You and your red flares of devotion blooming from the ironclad cage you call home, where the men reek of violent shit and the warfare of spilled blood. Where *vatos* and *veteranos* laugh, cry, ink each other's skin with the rusted afterthoughts of hieroglyphics. Kill each other. Love each other. Where time doesn't just stand still, rather chokes on the memories of a life once lived or never lived. Where the bars have no shadow because there is no sun. Where sound goes to disappear. In my mind I adorn your cell with the roses of *La Virgen de Morena*, place candles at your feet. Can you feel the heat of my prayers? Please come back to me.

El Duran, I am the soft dreamer, the tear-soaked believer. I'm slow jams without a lover, the loneliest place to be when the radio goes soft and the moon glow is all I got. I am poet without her poem. My *trenzas* weep as if willow, licorice black and dark night of grief. You are my caged crooner, *pinta profe* of romance, an incarcerated madness glowing hot. The cherry tip of a secreted *cigarillo*.

I will wait for Sundays for the rest of my life if I must, that torturous melancholy holy day. Call me purgatory. Call me limbo. Call me shadow woman of your dreams. I am *Malinche*, sacrificial flesh upon a *Mexica* altar. I will shower your letters with mascara-painted rain for all of history. *Por supuesto*, I will wait for you, *vato*. I have no choice. Our love is written in the stars, those smokey-eyed mirrors of my devout and pious faith. My relentless need for you. My homegirls cut me slack, though. They know I got it bad. Real bad. *Nuestro amor es la muerte. Nuestro amor es la vida.*

Siempre,
Sad Girl

PLEASE GOD, DON'T LET ME GROW UP
TO BE A CHOLA

Please God, don't let me grow up to be a Chola.
Grandma Mary says *sinvergüenzas* burn in hell
for all eternity and I don't even like the heat of June
when the summer comes down along our border town
as a guillotine does with no remorse.

Please God, don't let me grow up to be one of *those* women,
of fast fists, loose wombs, or dare I say, *mal floras*,
Cholas who love Cholas who kiss Cholas. I don't want to
smoke cigarettes in the back seat of a *firme* ride, all sparkle
'78 Chevy Impala. Or in the bathroom of Lulac Hall at Monique's
quinceanera the way Lupe and her homegirls do, smelling of Aqua Net, tobacco,
and Baby Soft perfume. The red-hot eyes of *demonias* glowing in the night.
I don't want to cavalier, dance until my hooves fall off, ink my body with the
stink of my hood. Let me be righteous. Let me be white-linen clean.

God, *mi diosa*, if I were to grow up to be a *Chola, cholita, chula*, high priestess
of all *putas*, at least let me be *La Jefa Ultima*. If I'm gonna do it, grow up to be a
Chola that is, give me all the wrath I was born for. All the love that the sun-
kissed, sun-drunk *Tonantzin* promised. Let me be *Tlatztoteotl*, filth eater and
spewer of poison.

But don't tell my grandma I prayed for this. Don't let her know about the
blood between my legs. How I boil at night. How my sleep purrs incantations.
Please, *tata dios*, let the Chola slide from me the way butter does from a too-hot
tortilla, all spittle and fleshy scorched dough. Let this sin unravel into the ether.
I'll take an egg, I promise, and wash the coolness over my *cabeza*, my chest, my
legs, like the good *curandera* Augustina does from down the street. *Limpias* $5
for all those who want to soap away their souls.

Without hex. Let my karma not be fouled by the mean streets. Last night an owl perched upon my windowsill. It cooed and crooned, *Baby, be who you are meant to be*. What does that mean, God? Was that a dream? A sugar-sprinkled *sueno*. My third eye tingled at the thought of it and I glowed, deep gold, and hovered above my bed. My *bruja* blood twitched.

Dear God, don't let me be a *bruja*, too in touch with her pain and magic. That is not the life for me. Or is it? A Chola with too much Chola for her own good.

Dear God, let me loosen this grip, set free this *fuerza* from my veins. This haunting from the house of my body.

Que Chola, oh Goddess, what have you done to me?

ALL CHOLA

for Mitch

You think you're all bad? Well, I'm badder.
I was made for sin. Cut from the cloth of Judas.
I'm all red tent and clothier of goddesses.
I weave tapestries for
the swagger of breast,
crotch,
legs short and *mean*
or long, lanky and *lean*.

I'm the seamstress for those who wield
knives or eyeliner, same difference.

I'm every part *bruja*, and no kinds of
repentance.

I don't pray on Sunday 'cept when I cruise,
a holy tabernacle on wheels.
I'm fin and tailspin. Your *locura* ain't got shit on me.

I'm the War Zone before it was renamed the International District.
You can't gentrify this.
Hey hipster, get your own *cultura*.

I'm allllll kinds of Chola, black as night without moon. Without stars.
I am the ink, bravado and braggadocious stink
of night. You got a light?

Let's smoke one more. Drink one more.
Dance once more and get 86'd from our not-so-favorite bar.
And if that *ruca* looks at my man one more time,
I'm gonna rip her fake-ass eyelashes from her face,
send an *I'm sorry* note to her grandma the next day.
Because that's how my mama raised me.

To do right when it feels good and wreck the night when it feels hood.
Door-knocker earrings swinging in the wind, like my fists,
like my love, like my mile-high heels dancing to my favorite song.

Sonrisa, as wide as the *sandia* sky cracking open the dawn.
Smile now and cry later, but only cry
when nobody sees you.

I'm all Chola, swagger and slink, wink of the eye-lined
kohl, jet-black ink as Nefferti did, raising empires and ziggurats
and babies. Fists in the air. *Chicana. Mexica. Mestiza.* Afro beauty and dreads.

You think you're all bad? Well, I'm badder.

A *bruja's* favorite hex.
The sex of me stitched in the helix of my DNA.
I am *Nepantla* woman.

El puño desnudo de mi amor enojado.
The naked fist of my angry love.

Mujer de sombra, woman of shadow
hiding in the bright, naked light.
For everyone to see even when they don't.
The in-between dream

you never saw coming.

FOUR

The Hood and Other Origin Stories

HOW REINA AND GINA GET READY
TO GO OUT (CIRCA 1988)

For the Paramount Party Girls of Long Beach

Hey, did we run out of the Agua Net, or what, aye?
> No *estúpida*, it's not Agua Net. It's Aqua Net.

Whatever tonta. Agua means water anyways. Aqua. Agua. It's all the same thing.
> *Cállate*, bitch. You don't know nothing. Just say it right.

Why, who cares?
> You want to go to college one day right?

Yeah.

> Then don't fuck up words, *pendeja*. The *pinche gueras* won't let you graduate.
Graduate? From where? High school or college?
> Both *idiota*.

Yeah, you right. Spencas, homegirl. Spencas. Wait. What do you mean gueras?
That sounds mighty racist of you, chavelita.

> Not all *gueras*, just those *gueras* who perpetuate institutional racism
> and stratification of our gente, therefore marginalizing people of color
> through means of cultural appropriation, politically positioned silencing tactics
> and other insidious forms of oppression. Duh. *En tiendas, mendas*?

Oh, well, yeah. Why didn't you just say that? Put that.
> Put that.

Besides, fuck them gueras.
> Yeah, fuck them *gueras*.

MALINALLI, GODDESS OF GRASS

for the hood

Mexica skies and green slivers of grass, armed to the teeth with medicine.
Individual soldiers set aflame with the chlorophyll of the creator's breath, cradle
the brown feet of mothers, magic-makers, copal-burning witchy women.

I could pull an oracle card from my kitchen table but I know what divinity
it speaks from the cloaked dark hut of the hearth of my home—it reads,
Outside, out there, is a majesty of movimiento and the modernity of tradition.

Babies still suckle the breast, pulling from the *tugforce* of life, *echo, echo, echo*
the *hoodstrife* of an urban landscape and the need for an oasis—sea green waves
of sedges, clades, and sprouted grain. We hold in our cupped palms the
forthcoming.

Here we sustain seven generations rising; find ritual in the pockets of the well-
manicured parks, the culs-de-sac, the tenements, the projects, the valleys and hills,
the five-point miracle, the place where urbanity meets land-based *musica*—and
las mujeres rejoice.

Our sashes dance in the breeze, red wind-whipped blood tattered but still here.
Our cotton skirts fan around our thighs, brown femurs connected to hip and bone.
Our hair pulled back testament to our battles and motherly connection to kin.

Zephyr. Gingham. Garb. Regalia. Kittel. Sacred threads and patchwork.

We rise in chorus and face the East. We are the neighborhood sirens, singing softly
with tongues made of steel, obsidian, minerals of the forgotten. We are the medicine
makers and melodious mamas. We hold this space for you.

We always, always forage the land.

THE KISS

for the hood

In the salt-soaked sweat crevices of the forefront of the crowned head,
chakra-drenched in gold, I kiss you here.

Here, I leave you this *receta de medicina*, a version of some love letter told to me
by the women before me and the women before that.

And all of the women who came before them.

Like Lucille Clifton wrote, we are *born in Babylon, both non-white and woman*,
so this is how we must survive the 'hood, exalt our songs, all crooked

angles and sword-heavy, but soft in the way we touch
each other. Our secreted language of *guerreras*, gilded tongues
and pouches of corn pollen adorn our neck.

For we have much to bear, pass on, and give.

Kinetic wire of transmission, magic-soaked *remedios* and we walk in beauty.
Or horror. Or trauma. Or lovelorn and lust. Or broken-hearted. Or hungry.
Ravenous. Raging. Relentless.

We are the dirge, the scorn, the first-born, the last-named, the stolen kiss.
The cradle. The croon. The moon. The mineral. The mothered and motherless.

Labios en la cabeza, dando la forma en que lo hacen los colibríes.

Reciprocating the way women do.
Taking and giving and taking and giving
the way women do.

RED-BREASTED AND BULLSEYE

after mixed-media on panel, Cardinal by Suzanne Sbarge

It's okay to fly red-breasted and heavy with bullseye milk
It is quite fine if your hair is aflame, crest of morning glory and blood sun
Fire-engine red and beak sharpened to a dagger
Not a common cardinal but rather a
songbird enchantress
a warrior avatar who whistles her knife-pitch song
an electric fence of sound to ward off perps and predators
to invite the lover home
or bid *adieu* to her brood
cleansing of the nest

Don't worry that your favorite cape is at the cleaners
baby birds sometimes regurgitate the regurgitated meals
lovingly funneled down the sleeve of their throats
It's the way of parenthood, superhero swagger
besides you can make anything look fly

(that was a play on words)

We are all built with our totems stitched into the seams of our dreams
our flights and fancies, our feathered quills
the red blood that pulsates beneath the thin
veil of our eyelids
membrane of eggshell
uterus glow

We must transform and transform again
shed the mutable skins of life
we must embark the holy metamorphosis
sprout beaks and clutching claw

We must come into animal presence
and us into them

become the beastly goddess
root around the fragrant dirt
slice through dawn and dusk
with kamikaze letters writ
upon your feathered underbelly

dive-bomb those who would hurt you or those you bore
pierce their ears with song and siren
love forever

And lest you forget
Remember that you wear red well
the bullseye a birthmark
a talisman from the gods

Proving yourself worthy
time and time again

THE ARREST OF THE PALETEROS

after Frank Romero
for the hood

When they came for the *paleteros* the folx wondered at the lack of their song,
and the hood was without bells and chimes and the lilt-soft Spanish dialect
of an Oaxacan *tongue*.

Or Zacateco.
Or Juarense.
Guanajuato.
Michoacán.

Sugar-spun *fresa* and the tang of *lima con chamoy* simply drifted by,
up into the air and disappeared,
Huitzil wings fading into the soft summer air.
The sun still blazed high.

They came for the *paleteros.*
They beat them with batons and bricks.
They loosened their pockets
for *papeles* and permits.

And the ICE agents came and came and took them away.

They took them away in cuffs. And the windowless, unmarked vans
snapped their jowls around sun-weathered bodies, their
thick brown hands, their rusted skin, deep as an oxidized stone.
The Uncles. The Grandfathers. The Fathers. The Brothers.

They took them away.

The afternoon is a red-hot scimitar, a juggler of swords.
Heat rising in bending waves from the grassless hood, and the air
stinks of black-tarred streets, of steaming potholes.

But here come los *paleteros*, streamers and colored mirrors,
circus dreams and coconut-slivered popsicles, coins jangling in
pockets, stashed away in hopeful socks and mamas' purses.

We ride away on the dreams of our delighted taste buds.
Fantastic voyages of sweet summer afternoons, the way memories
should be made. We pray to these migrating
mosques of ice blocks and frozen treats.

We all run out into the heat, hood-hubs and corner streets,
waving our dollars and cupping coins, dizzy with the chant,
the call the of *paletero*—

Paletas! Paletas!
      Paletas de Mango!
            Paletas de aguacate!

Paletas de fresa y crema!
      Paletas de chocolate! De chicle rosa!
            Almendra! Amaretto! De cocoa!
Paletas!

Until the song sings like a summer hood siren, no more.
Until everyone marvels at the lack of song.

The lack of *sabor en la lengua*. The taste of summer
on the tongue,
gone.

The bodies, the brown bodies,
the bodies disappeared.

MANMADE MATERIALS

The chain-link knows nothing of beating hearts, of lax
flesh or parting fingers. Knows nothing of separation.
How it splits a mother's chest open like *manzana*
beneath a sutured knife. Juice of the blood. How
a father becomes impotent because politicians
are in bed with the businessmen. And brown bodies
turn a profit when they are behind fences.

How babies are interned. *How brown babies are interned.*

The chain-link and the aluminum blankets can't hear.
They have neither ears nor eyes. No sight. Only
malleable chemistry to be fashioned, shaped as
accoutrements for the incarcerated child-bodies,
round up and laid out upon the slabs of pavement.

The pavement never remembers.

The paper doesn't know if it is a green card or not.
Doesn't know the difference between a passport
and a deportation warrant. It certainly doesn't care
if it is a page in the bible or a constitution.

The desert is just a desert. In all its glittering,
thirsty glory. It was merely born that way. It never
knew and will never know about manmade borders.

A prison is only a collection of angles and hooked wire.
It doesn't understand it was meant to be a cell.
A cell is unknowing of itself. It cannot recognize grief.

All of the keys and all of the locks in this world
will never suffer. But metal can be a dangerous
thing. This we know.

We know that men, in the name of power
and devotion to the coin, will eat the poor
for dinner. Will place us on plates of gold. Tuck
the linen into the starch of the collar. Wet
their lips with the blood of the guiltless and call
us a delicacy.

Their wives will exclaim over the recipe,
the exotic snuff of it. Pick their pearly whites
with our bones.

We know. I know, they gobble the spirit of their
brothers and sisters never to
acknowledge us as kin.

This is how animal becomes less than human.
How a human is less than the blood it was born in.
Less than machine and metal and tool.

This is how their teeth are akin to chain-link.
Their tongues, a paper ballot, the ink that runs
from the sides of their mouths as they chew.
Masticate their jaws. Pay their dinner bill with plastic.

The ones who own everything. Who own
the mineral, the land, the stainless-steel toilets
in all of the prisons. Who think they own you.

Who don't understand that the heart is a
manzana. An apple that grew from the tree
but was never enslaved by it. The branch is
a benevolent passenger.

This is how an apple is different from chain-link.
How, in this knowledge, the meek, the righteous,
will one day inherit the earth.

when I was a young poet of no consequence
but not really a poet because I was only an undergrad student
enrolled in a not-that-quite-renowned university of words I
questioned my poetry instructor's reading selection one afternoon

she read aloud to us her trite and soft pink tongue
wagging along on some watered-down Wednesday
of no particular distinction

it was a poem by some white lady who may or may not have already died and it
was about springtime bulbs bursting from the coffee-colored
dirt of her backyard garden I could smell the dirt the white flesh of the worm
the mycelium like an afterbirth the poem was that good and also not that good
at that time I was bored and indignant rebellious and hopped up on young sex
and dormitory drugs snorted the weekend before or the weekend before that

which is to say that I thought I was wise
beyond my years and in many ways I really was

and so I said I said I said to the instructor that this poem seems
notwithstanding your own personal interest disinteresting and what
is the point who cares of those vain and lonely blooming petals
destined to die in some white lady's backyard anyway and where
is the revolution where is the boycott where are the brown and black
bodies and the blood and the bullets and the pain of all of
our childhoods

who cares for those soon-to-be-inconsequential wilting flowers
why bother with those short stanzas and too-little line lengths there is no
ritmo or *ganas* and where is the hip-swivel of sex give me dynamite give me
guernica where is the war the struggle Pablo's postman the sit-in the walk-out
the effigy and *justicia*

and she a bitter but hardened battle-axe teacher only decades of teaching
poetry to sex-juiced college kids can afford said in all of her
affluent and privileged white-knuckled knowledge said so she said
she said that the struggle of life my dear
and the nucleus of war and all the legacy of biblical bloodshed can be found
in the birthing of a flower in the mysterious caul of the seed in the dying of
what was once a thirsting and reaching-for-life
naïve bud the bulb the birth the beauteous beckoning
in the snow-crust and wind-whipped seasonal change and in all of the ways
a stalk a leaf and sometimes even the root lives if lucky if coerced convinced
convened waving its stubborn flag and then and then she said she
said as suddenly as it lives it dies
dies she said

just wait and watch in all of the ways you will grow old dear when your
tits touch the ground and your heart is a thing of paper less than paper
I will be long gone but you you she said she said you and this poem will
still be alive for at least a bit love at least a bit dancing the
way boxers dance in the ring fighting to survive someone else's game
the tale of the tape sweating and pulsing praying to matter survive mean
something to someone somewhere along the way

she said she said then to me she said then read it again
read the damned and ephemeral poem again dear she said

wait and watch fight for life or not in any case retribution will be mine
will be mine dear finally finally the poem will reveal itself

I remember how I finally grew convinced with her conviction
and thought this is what I thought that it was a gift my listening
how generous I was in my understanding

I remember how she thought she never thought twice to acknowledge me
and my swaggering arrogant *alivewithblood* words and that that I say that
too I will always remember

A PANTOUM FOR BREONNA

after Theodre Roethke
for the Hood

Was she dreaming in the moments before she died, sleep-heavy memory-pulse of
    the brain?
And if she dreamt, was it of a rocking chair or a swing that swung in the air
    of her childhood?
How, in the terror of the battering ram, did she wake, guns spitting bullets her
    way?
And fuck a no-knock warrant and fuck their mistake, muted rage of fear, ferocity,
    and foul play.

And if she dreamt, was it of a rocking chair or a swing that swung in the air
    of her childhood?
Did roses bloom like bullet holes from the body, vermillion and spilling onto
    the rug?
Did she foretell in the dream images of her deep sleep that a violent squall neared
    her door?
Did she wake to sleep and take her waking slow?

Did roses bloom like bullet holes from the body, vermillion and spilling onto
    the rug?
Eight shots, ringing, ringing, ringing, thrusting headfirst into the air, that
    dark-spun night.
andthebloodandthebloodandthebloodandthebloodandthe—bright petals
    of a turning rose.
Did she feel her fate in what she feared and did she take her waking slow?

Eight shots, ringing, ringing, ringing, thrusting head first into the air, that dark-
    spun night.
And how I hope her last dream she dreamt was made of light, crystal stairwell to
    the unknown.
And fuck a no-knock warrant, and fuck a suspect and fuck a white man's lament.
How I hoped she dreamed of something sweet, something slow. Something.
    Something. Slow.

SHOOTING HOOPS IN THE HOOD
AND HALLELUJAH WE BALL

for the hood

Shooting hoops in the hood and hallelujah we ball, fast-break
finger-roll magic tricks as a hook-shot kisses the brim, sinks
like a slow orange, leather-clad sun into the horizon.

We are the high-dribble priesthood, the slam dunk of a summer
afternoon broke open, dancers and gliders of the tarmac.

Acolytes, worshippers of asphalt.

We, the brotherly love of an incomplete team and so we two-step,
wings on our feet and flutter like levitating magicians above the
neighborhood courts. We, the juke-footed jesters of the rebound.
The courtesans rising, royalty of our own making. We the kings, pharaohs,
prophets, and medicine men of the free throw, the way it finds the hole—

three points closer to god. Icarus soaring, heliotrope-honied skies kissing our
waxen wings but *the heat can't fuck with this.*

We are the sun, the wind, and the elements of a boundless sky, flying high,
flying high, and there is a freedom here of our own device.

We are bank-shot, blocked-shot, shit-talkers of the court. We who palm
the whole wide world in our hands, chest pass and pass back,
jump shots and layups.

Grande Jeté, plié, pirouette, ballet.

Shooting hoops in the hood
and *hallelujah* we ball.

Hallelujah, how we ball.

I HOSTED A PARTY

We lit a fire of cedar and my gasoline-soaked
ex-husband's underwear.

Jasmine spoke of steaming her vagina with rose
petal and lavender water.

Ebony was a messy spine but still she stood erect, right there, next
to my dirty stove. Eva had bottom surgery last fall and her thighs sang

in gratitude, a wet whistle like a red-breasted bird. I cried because I had
drank too much wine. Cabernet makes me weepy. It was New Year's Eve

and the best harpies came to visit.
It was a ceremony of good-byes.

Violet scissored pictures of women from the stack of Playboy magazines
piled atop my kitchen table and pasted them to colorful sheets of

construction paper. Red, merrywinkle, pusce, and faded bits of blue
stock card. Nipples sprinkled across the floor. Every one of us was a

vision board. Not Amanda, though. She could not
make it. Her babysitter had canceled. I remember her absence

as if she were there.
We were nine and not ten.

We took a group photo that night. Katrina's sweater was drunk and slipped
over her shoulder. In the picture her right breast gleams like the pearl

in Vermeer's painting. I look not unhappy. This is a good memory. And outside
in my backyard the fire burned under a pregnant winter moon. The air was brisk

and we ate cheese and Mediterranean olives that Brooke had brought
to my party. Brooke was quiet as usual. A blonde mystery with eyes that said

everything she didn't want to. Who else was there? Oh yes, Anna,
all salt-and-pepper hair, newly shorn and lusty. She read Tarot but I don't

remember what cards she pulled for me.
I had moved on to sipping silver tequila from a clay mug.

The night was a wintery negligee. I do recall how one by one
we joined the fire. We were rage and melancholia,

and so of course, the fire beckoned to us. That loopy siren.
Yöeme cracked jokes and stoked the fire. Her laughter was a tree branch.

A reverberating *maraca* in love with the stage. We inched our way
down the backyard stoop, past my crooked concrete stairs

without rail, bypassed the overgrown weeds and frost and cool air.
We became coterie. Became lanterns. Became mothlike creatures

in our collective pain. She and she and her and her inhaled our delicious
tears and made joy out of it. Riley had the biggest smile

of them all. She had expelled all of the bullshit years before.
She gleamed as a virgin does. We made an effigy of her. Her cheeks

apple-red and robust mirrors to the flames.
We see the dusty face of *Tonantzin* in the fire.

The reaper waves her flag but we say no to her advances.
Not here, not tonight, dear long-jowled sweet one. Orishas spit

and dance their way out of the embers. They are roving blazing jewels.
The wine is a jealous lover in our glasses and we suck her dry.

The emerald heat of it held our rapture.
The clock struck midnight, and as all good witches do,

we join in chorus and our laments shook the moon
from the sky. Our idols rattled in their graves as we howled.

Wild sleek things. Howling like bitches in heat.
Like a pack of dying mothers, letting go.

In the new year,
we finally let go.

FIVE *After the Words*

TLALOC

Across the street from my house breathes a cemetery, old dirt and mounds of marble and the dead huddle waiting for me. I tend not to notice that which does not live. I call this fear and nostril-heavy neglect of what will become of my mortal coil. This is how I survive Wednesday.

Tlaloc begins to weep, sweeping across the valley, and fills the ditches with its jeremiad wetness. I can smell the dirt, which is to write, I smell the dead. How they toil in their sarcophaguses, entombed shrines of formaldehyde; chemicals that keep the not-alive bodies tidy. I feel sorry for those burrowed arms and legs and heads, never able to reach the roots of trees or become chum for the beetle bug.

I hear it is illegal to bury a body beneath a tree without the proper paperwork and I wonder who will do me that favor when I expire? I tell all of my living kin and foe, to please dig a ditch. Lower this body beneath a tree. Or at least a shrub.

Let Tlaloc rain upon me until I melt, gelatinous biology into the dirt. Glorious sufferer of the beetle bugs. Tlaloc will know what to do with the left-behinds. I fear no one is listening.

Indeed some well-intentioned soul will embalm me. Let the coroner crack open my skull, my sternum, place my bowels and organs on a cold, digital scale. Write down the dimensions of my insides that will be logged into the annals of this city's paperwork of the expired. No one will ever research my life. That is fine, but let me be *freefreefree*. Give me a tree. A sagebrush. A forgotten rosemary bundle.

No one will recall how I yearn for the rain to set me free. For my body to be allowed to become the disparate carbon it is meant to be. Tlaloc will rain down upon some cold stone that is etched with the summarized biography of my life. Here lies her. The she-demon who cannot be purged from her sins. Here she will roll around in her gray casket forever and ever. A harpie captive within a bullet-shaped coffin too expensive for its own good. Glossy with its modernity.

And the rain will not shine upon her bones. How sad,
I think that the rain will not wetten these bones.

PINNACLE

I dreamt I drowned and in that pinnacle
of watery life
ending in death beginning in birth,
my heart was a jade apple.

No, that is not how I want to start this poem.

The apple was a chamber of pistons, porous white flesh
imprisoned by the scarlet skin wet on the tongue.

Cinnabar.
Garnet.
Bixbite.

I ate my own heart the way my *Mexica* ancestors sliced
open the sacrificial skin of the sternum, surgical sharp and saturated
with primordial rage, pulled the blood of their enemies
that rivered their bodies and commenced to cannibalize the spirit.
I ate it like that.

Ruby.
Topaz.
Tourmaline.

Wait, I regret that attempted first line too. Let me try again.

Something less violent convinces me to shape an image
that does not involve blood or tongue or genocide.
But that would not be a truth I know.

My last attempt to begin this poem.

Here is a beginning with less
choking, for you, *O'*
soft-hearted readers.

I will lie to you in honor of you.

I dreamt a variation of things like Langston did,
where the cool wind swept in and baptized my forehead.

Yes, let me be renaissance and pale swift branches
vibrating beneath a springtime moon.

I will be soft for you dear-hearted listener because drowning
is a quick-fire way to lose the ear.

Red-breasted apple.
Fire Opal.
Blood Jaspar.

No.

Moonstone.
Mother of Pearl.
Goshenite.

And.

White Diamond.
Milk Quartz.
Alabaster Eye of the Sapphire.

Yes.

This poem is an ear.
It is someone listening
for a verse to begin.
Light as a ripple.
Light the way linen touches the flesh is,
right before the best dream you ever dreamt
drops from the tree,
ripe with the fruit of hope.

Yes, let me start the poem like this:

Hope. Here is hope.

NOTES

"Our Transgression": The italicized lines that make up stanza five are from Algernon Charles Swinburne's "Love and Sleep."

"The First and Last Pain": The last line is from Sharon Old's poem "Material Ode."

"The Kiss": The italicized text comes from Lucille Clifton's poem "won't you celebrate with me."